COUNTRY  PROFILES

# HUNGARY

BY ALICIA Z. KLEPEIS

BELLWETHER MEDIA • MINNEAPOLIS, MN

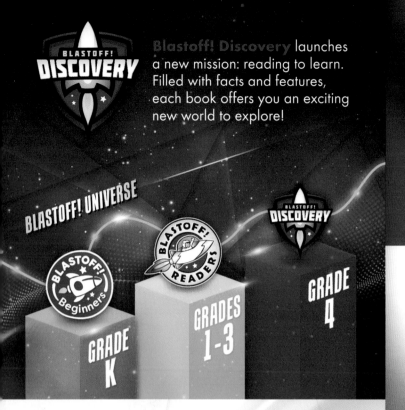

**Blastoff! Discovery** launches a new mission: reading to learn. Filled with facts and features, each book offers you an exciting new world to explore!

BLASTOFF! UNIVERSE

BLASTOFF! Beginners
GRADE K

BLASTOFF! READERS
GRADES 1-3

BLASTOFF! DISCOVERY
GRADE 4

This edition first published in 2023 by Bellwether Media, Inc.

No part of this publication may be reproduced in whole or in part without written permission of the publisher.
For information regarding permission, write to Bellwether Media, Inc., Attention: Permissions Department,
6012 Blue Circle Drive, Minnetonka, MN 55343.

Library of Congress Cataloging-in-Publication Data

Names: Klepeis, Alicia, 1971- author.
Title: Hungary / by Alicia Z. Klepeis.
Description: Minneapolis : Bellwether Media, 2023. | Series: Country
    profiles | Includes bibliographical references and index. |
    Audience: Ages 7-13 | Audience: Grades 4-6 | Summary:
    "Engaging images accompany information about Hungary.
    The combination of high-interest subject matter and narrative text is
    intended for students in grades 3 through 8"–Provided by publisher.
Identifiers: LCCN 2022016479 (print) | LCCN 2022016480 (ebook)
    | ISBN 9781644877470 (library binding) | ISBN
    9781648347931 (ebook)
Subjects: LCSH: Hungary–Juvenile literature.
Classification: LCC DB906 .K55 2023  (print) | LCC DB906  (ebook)
    | DDC 943.9–dc23/eng/20220414
LC record available at https://lccn.loc.gov/2022016479
LC ebook record available at https://lccn.loc.gov/2022016480

Editor: Rebecca Sabelko     Designer: Brittany McIntosh

Printed in the United States of America, North Mankato, MN.

# TABLE OF CONTENTS

A family starts their adventure in Budapest at the Castle Museum. They walk along the museum's red marble floor. Giant paintings reveal Hungary's past. The kids touch fabrics like those that once covered the walls. After the museum, the family follows the cobblestone streets to Matthias Church. They listen to organ music before heading to lunch.

## OTHER TOP SITES

AGGTELEK NATIONAL PARK

HUNGARIAN PARLIAMENT BUILDING

LAKE HÉVÍZ

SOPRON TOWN HALL

A cormorant dives into the Danube River as the family arrives at Margaret Island. While on the island, they rent bikes and visit the Japanese garden. At dusk, they watch the grand fountain's music and lights show. Welcome to Hungary!

Hungary is a nation in central Europe. It covers an area of 35,918 square miles (93,028 square kilometers). The country's capital, Budapest, stands in north-central Hungary. The Danube River divides the city into two parts. Buda lies on the west bank. Pest stands on the east bank.

Hungary is **landlocked**. Austria is its northwestern neighbor. Slovakia forms much of Hungary's northern border. Ukraine lies to the northeast. The southeastern border with Romania is long. The Danube River flows though Hungary into its southern neighbor, Serbia. Croatia and Slovenia stand to the southwest and west.

AUSTRIA

SLOVENIA

CROATIA

SLOVAKIA

UKRAINE

MISKOLC

DEBRECEN

★ - - - BUDAPEST

HUNGARY

SZEGED

ROMANIA

● - - - PÉCS

SERBIA

# LANDSCAPE AND CLIMATE

Lowlands make up much of Hungary. The Little Hungarian **Plain** is in the northwest. Low mountains run along the southeastern edge of this **fertile** area. The larger Great Hungarian Plain covers most of central and southeastern Hungary.

The Danube River flows south through the middle of the country. Farmers in eastern Hungary depend on the Tisza River to help water their crops.

LAKE BALATON

## ONE BIG LAKE

Located in western Hungary, Lake Balaton is the nation's largest lake. People sail and bird-watch on its waters. They also hike along its shores.

TISZA RIVER
GREAT HUNGARIAN PLAIN

**BUDAPEST**

**Average seasonal highs and lows**

**JANUARY**
HIGH: 34 °F (1 °C)
LOW: 25 °F (-4 °C)

**APRIL**
HIGH: 61 °F (16 °C)
LOW: 43 °F (6 °C)

**JULY**
HIGH: 81 °F (27 °C)
LOW: 59 °F (15 °C)

**OCTOBER**
HIGH: 61 °F (16 °C)
LOW: 45 °F (7 °C)

°F = degrees Fahrenheit
°C = degrees Celsius

Hungary's climate is **continental**. Winters are cold and summers are hot. The nation's driest areas are in the Great Hungarian Plain. Much of the year's rain falls during the growing season.

In Hungary's mountain forests, wild boars search for fruits and roots. Red deer feed on shrubs. In the lowlands, rodents and hares hide from buzzards searching for a meal.
Gray partridges make nests and dig for food on the ground. Bream, carp, and pike are some of the many fish that swim in Hungary's rivers and lakes.

Hortobágy National Park is home to a wide variety of animals. Herds of wild horses graze on grasses during the day. Foxes hunt for birds and small mammals at night. Thousands of cranes stop in the park on their **migration** south.

COMMON
BUZZARD

WILD BOAR

RED DEER

## TERRIFIC TOADS

Fire-bellied toads can be found in many freshwater areas in Hungary. They are known for their bright orange bellies. This color can warn enemies that their skin is poisonous.

GRAY
PARTRIDGE

# GRAY PARTRIDGE

Life Span: up to 5 years
Red List Status: least concern

gray partridge range =

| LEAST CONCERN | NEAR THREATENED | VULNERABLE | ENDANGERED | CRITICALLY ENDANGERED | EXTINCT IN THE WILD | EXTINCT |
|---|---|---|---|---|---|---|

Hungary is home to nearly 10 million people. Over 8 out of 10 are part of the Hungarian **ethnic** group. The Roma, whose **ancestors** came from northern India, are the second-largest group. Germans make up a small part of the population. More than 200,000 **migrants** live in Hungary.

Over half of all Hungarians are Christian. Most other people do not practice any religion. Almost everyone in Hungary speaks Hungarian. It is the nation's official language. English and German are commonly spoken, too.

## FAMOUS FACE

Name: Harry Houdini
Birthday: March 24, 1874
Died: October 31, 1926
Hometown: Budapest, Hungary
Famous for: One of the most famous magicians in history, known for his grand illusions and daring escape acts

## SPEAK HUNGARIAN

| ENGLISH | HUNGARIAN | HOW TO SAY IT |
|---|---|---|
| hello | szia | SEE-ya |
| goodbye | viszontlátásra | VEE-sont-la-ta-shra |
| please | kérem | KAY-rem |
| thank you | köszönöm | KUH-suh-num |
| yes | igen | EE-ghen |
| no | nem | nem |

BUDAPEST

## A SPECIAL NUMBER

No building in Budapest can be taller than 96 meters (315 feet). This is because 96 is a meaningful number in Hungary. In 896 CE, the early stages of the Hungarian Kingdom began.

More than 7 out of 10 Hungarians live in **urban** areas. Nearly 2 million people dwell in Hungary's largest city, Budapest. Most Hungarians live in small apartments. People often take the subway, **trams**, or buses to get around. They also bike when traveling short distances.

Families in **rural** areas often live in houses. Their living spaces are larger than in cities. Country homes commonly have food gardens. Buses connect rural areas with cities. Many Hungarians in the countryside also travel by car.

Hungary has a rich folk art **tradition**. Hungarian folk pottery features detailed designs and bright colors. Most kitchens have pottery on display. Ceiling and wall paintings enrich homes and churches. People celebrate all kinds of music. Franz Liszt is one of the country's most famous classical composers. Béla Bartók brought folk music to a wider audience.

Young people in Hungary often wear jeans. Businesspeople tend to wear suits. Traditional dress is sometimes worn in rural areas or for special occasions. Women may wear **embroidered** skirts and blouses. Men wear vests. The patterns and colors can vary by region.

Children in Hungary must begin kindergarten at age 3. They attend basic schools from ages 6 to 14. Secondary school normally lasts four years. Some schools prepare students for college. If students do well on an exam, they can study at a university. Other schools teach specific job skills.

Nearly two out of three Hungarians have **service jobs**. Many work in the **tourism** industry. They have jobs in hotels, museums, and parks. Factories in Hungary produce vehicle parts, cars, medicines, and **textiles**. Farmers grow wheat, maize, beets, and barley. **Organic** farming is growing quickly.

FACTORY

### SOUR CHERRIES

Hungary is one of the world's top producers of sour cherries. They taste tart. Most people make them into jams, pies, or other baked goods.

FENCING

The most popular sport in Hungary is soccer. Children regularly play at school. Fans cheer on the nation's professional teams. Hungarians also enjoy basketball, swimming, and **fencing**. People take part in many outdoor activities such as sailing and fishing. Popular hiking spots include the Matra Mountains and Bükk National Park.

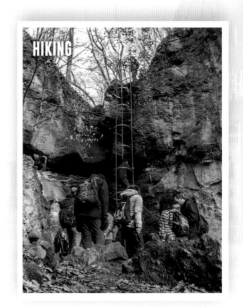

HIKING

Many Hungarians go to concerts or museums in their free time. They also meet friends for afternoon tea or dessert at cafés. **Thermal baths** created from hot springs are popular. People enjoy relaxing in these pools. Some spas also have wave pools or beaches.

THERMAL BATHS

# SQUIRREL WITHOUT A HOUSE GAME

Hungary has many fun games for children. This one can be played in any large space. The more players, the merrier!

## What You Need:

- hula hoops, one less than the number of players, or chalk
- a whistle

## How to Play:

1. If you are using hula hoops, spread them out on the ground. You can draw circles on the ground if you do not have enough hula hoops. The hoop or chalk circle represents a squirrel's house.

2. To start the game, one person will be the leader. They are in charge of the whistle.

3. The leader will blow the whistle and shout out, "Squirrels, run out of your houses! One, two, three!" During this time the players have to run around to find a hoop or circle to step into. When the leader blows the whistle, whichever player has no hoop is a squirrel without a house and is out.

4. Before the next round begins, one hoop is removed from play.

5. Repeat steps 3 and 4 until only one player is left inside a hoop. They are the winner!

GOULASH

## SWEET SOUPS

Hungarian cooks make many kinds of fruit soup. The most popular is chilled sour cherry soup. These sweet soups are served before the main course, not as dessert.

Breakfast in Hungary often includes sandwiches, cold meats, and cheeses. Pastries like the chocolaty *kakaós csiga* are also popular. Many meals feature meat and the spice paprika. One example is goulash. This beef and vegetable stew is the national dish. People also often eat stuffed cabbage leaves or peppers. Fillings are beef or pork, rice, and tomatoes.

*Lángos* is a favorite snack in Hungary. It is fried dough with sour cream and cheese on top. One popular dessert is *krémes*. This treat is made of puff pastry and thick cream. *Dobos torte* is a cake topped with caramel.

KAKAÓS CSIGA

DOBOS TORTE

# HUNGARIAN MUSHROOM SOUP

Have an adult help you make this savory soup!

Ingredients:

1/2 stick (4 tablespoons) unsalted butter
2 cups onions, chopped
1 pound mushrooms, sliced
2 teaspoons dried dill
1 tablespoon paprika
1 tablespoon soy sauce
2 cups vegetable or chicken broth
1 cup milk (not skim)
3 tablespoons flour
2 teaspoons lemon juice
1/4 cup fresh parsley, chopped
1/2 cup sour cream
salt and pepper, to taste

Steps:

1. In a big pot, melt the butter over medium heat. Add the onions and cook for 5 minutes. Add the mushrooms and cook for 5 more minutes. Add the dill, paprika, soy sauce, and broth. Turn the heat down to low and cover the pot. Cook for 15 minutes.

2. In a small bowl, whisk together the milk and flour. Pour this mixture into the soup pot. Stir until well combined. Cover the pot again and cook for another 15 minutes, stirring occasionally.

3. Add the lemon juice, parsley, and sour cream to the soup. Stir to combine and cook on low heat for 3 to 5 minutes.

4. Add salt and pepper to taste. Serve right away. Enjoy!

REVOLUTION
DAY

Hungarians celebrate Revolution Day on March 15.
This holiday marks the day a war for independence began
against the Austrian Empire. Concerts and speeches are
common events. Christians often celebrate Easter by going
to church and visiting with family. They also decorate eggs
and enjoy a feast.

August 20 is Saint Stephen's Day. People remember Hungary's first king, Saint Stephen. They also bake bread to mark the arrival of the harvest. Christmas is a festive time of year. Markets light up squares throughout Budapest. Hungarians celebrate their **culture** and traditions all year long!

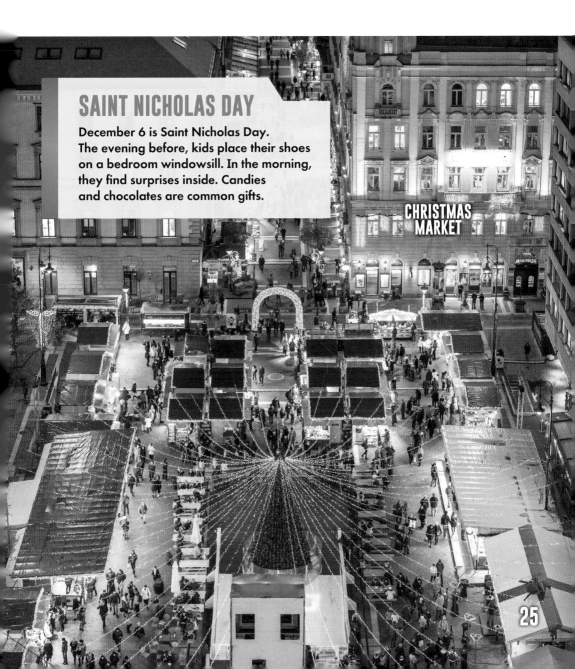

## SAINT NICHOLAS DAY

December 6 is Saint Nicholas Day. The evening before, kids place their shoes on a bedroom windowsill. In the morning, they find surprises inside. Candies and chocolates are common gifts.

CHRISTMAS MARKET

**1367**
Hungary's first university is founded at Pécs

**9TH CENTURY**
The Magyars, or Hungarian-speaking people, settle the Danube Plain in what is now Hungary

**1918**
Hungary gains independence after centuries of rule by the Austrian Hapsburgs

**1526**
Ottoman Turks take control over most of Hungary until 1699

**1000**
Stephen I becomes the first king of Hungary

**1919**
Communists take power over Hungary

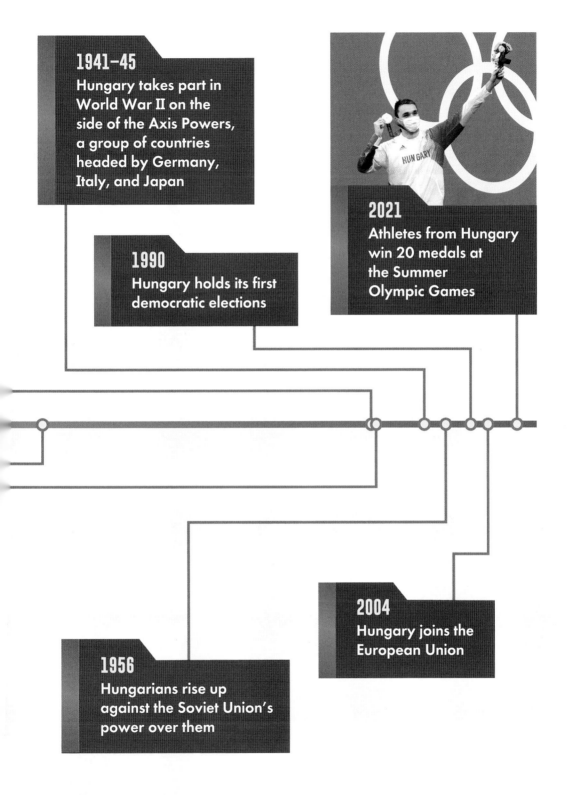

**1941–45**
Hungary takes part in World War II on the side of the Axis Powers, a group of countries headed by Germany, Italy, and Japan

**2021**
Athletes from Hungary win 20 medals at the Summer Olympic Games

**1990**
Hungary holds its first democratic elections

**2004**
Hungary joins the European Union

**1956**
Hungarians rise up against the Soviet Union's power over them

**Official Name:** Hungary

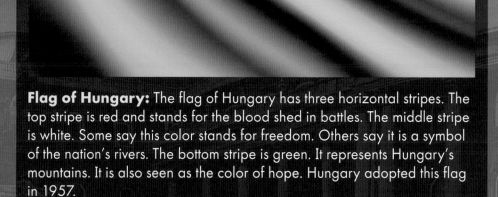

**Flag of Hungary:** The flag of Hungary has three horizontal stripes. The top stripe is red and stands for the blood shed in battles. The middle stripe is white. Some say this color stands for freedom. Others say it is a symbol of the nation's rivers. The bottom stripe is green. It represents Hungary's mountains. It is also seen as the color of hope. Hungary adopted this flag in 1957.

**Area:** 35,918 square miles
(93,028 square kilometers)

**Capital City:** Budapest

**Important Cities:** Debrecen, Szeged, Miskolc, Pécs

**Population:**
9,699,577 (2022 est.)

COUNTRYSIDE
**27.4%**

**WHERE PEOPLE LIVE**

CITY
**72.6%**

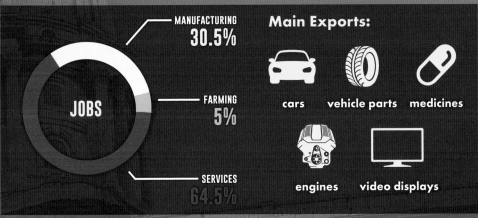

**MANUFACTURING**
**30.5%**

**JOBS**

**FARMING**
**5%**

**SERVICES**
**64.5%**

**Main Exports:**

cars    vehicle parts    medicines

engines    video displays

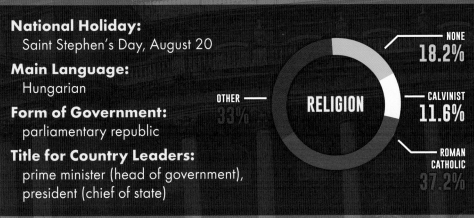

**National Holiday:**
Saint Stephen's Day, August 20

**Main Language:**
Hungarian

**Form of Government:**
parliamentary republic

**Title for Country Leaders:**
prime minister (head of government),
president (chief of state)

**RELIGION**

OTHER
33%

**NONE**
**18.2%**

**CALVINIST**
**11.6%**

**ROMAN CATHOLIC**
**37.2%**

**Unit of Money:**
Hungarian forint

# GLOSSARY

**ancestors**—relatives who lived a long time ago

**continental**—related to a relatively dry climate with very cold winters and very hot summers

**culture**—the beliefs, arts, and ways of life in a place or society

**embroidered**—decorated with patterns sewn on with thread

**ethnic**—related to a group of people who share customs and an identity

**fencing**—a sport that involves fighting with swords where participants try to score points against opponents

**fertile**—able to support growth

**landlocked**—completely surrounded by land

**migrants**—people who have moved to a new place for work or who have been forced to leave their home

**migration**—the process of moving from one place to another, often with the seasons

**organic**—referring to farming that does not use pesticides or chemical fertilizers

**plain**—a large area of flat land

**rural**—related to the countryside

**service jobs**—jobs that perform tasks for people or businesses

**textiles**—fabrics that are woven or knit

**thermal baths**—places to soak that use the water from hot springs; hot springs are areas where warm water flows out of the ground.

**tourism**—the business of people traveling to visit other places

**tradition**—a custom, idea, or belief handed down from one generation to the next

**trams**—passenger vehicles powered by electricity from an overhead cable

**urban**—related to cities and city life

# TO LEARN MORE

## AT THE LIBRARY

Bisson, Michelle. *Hedy's Journey: The True Story of a Hungarian Girl Fleeing the Holocaust.* North Mankato, Minn.: Capstone Press, 2017.

Meir, Tamar. *Francesco Tirelli's Ice Cream Shop.* Minneapolis, Minn.: Kar-Ben Publishing, 2019.

Spanier, Kristine. *Hungary.* Minneapolis, Minn.: Jump!, 2022.

## ON THE WEB

# FACTSURFER

Factsurfer.com gives you a safe, fun way to find more information.

1. Go to www.factsurfer.com.

2. Enter "Hungary" into the search box and click 🔍.

3. Select your book cover to see a list of related content.

# INDEX

The images in this book are reproduced through the courtesy of: Mirelle, front cover; Yasonya, pp. 4-5; Tainar, p. 5 (Aggtelek National Park); V_E, p. 5 (Hungarian Parliament Building); kaiser-v, p. 5 (Lake Hévíz); Votimedia, p. 5 (Sopron town hall); vidalgo, p. 8; Zeljko Radojko, p. 9 (top); ZGPhotography, p. 9 (bottom); WildMedia, p. 10 (buzzard); McGraw, p. 10 (boar); Paolo-manzi, p. 10 (deer); Kirsanov Valeriy Vladimirovich, p. 10 (toad); Kit Day/ Alamy, p. 10-11; Soul, p. 12; Chronicle/ Alamy, p. 13 (top); photo.ua, p. 13 (bottom); S-F, p. 14; manasesistvan, p. 15; Andocs, pp. 15, 16; Noemi Bruzak/ AP Images, p. 18; Bloomberg/ Contributor/ Getty, p. 19 (top); Evgeniia Biriukova/ Alamy, p. 19 (middle); Tim UR, p. 19 (bottom); Marco Ciccolella, p. 20 (top); Gelefin, p. 20 (bottom); Izabela23, p. 21 (top); StaislauV, p. 21 (bottom); frantic/ Alamy, p. 22 (top); Mike Laptev, p. 22 (bottom); Nikoletta Lia Muhari, p. 23 (top); AlenaKogotkova, p. 23 (middle); AS Food studio, p. 23 (bottom); Reuters/ Alamy, p. 24; Calin Stan, p. 25; history_docu_photo/ Alamy, p. 26; Independent Photo Agency/ Alamy, p. 27; Clad Breazu/ Alamy, p. 29 (banknote); Arsgera, p. 29 (coin).